My First
Book of Prayers

CATHOLIC EDITION

Written by
Daniel J. Porter
and
Rev. Victor Hoagland, C.P.

Edited by
Debbie Butcher Wiersma

Illustrated by
Samuel J. Butcher

MRP

The Regina Press
New York

Presented to_____

by_____

on_____

This book is dedicated to the memory of Edmond C. Malhame, our father, our friend, and our mentor. Without your inspiration, love, and guidance, The Regina Press would not exist. We will never forget you and will proudly carry on your legacy.

George and Robert

Thank You for being with me
today and every day.
I know You're always with me...
I know You think of me even
when I'm not thinking of You.
Sometimes I like to talk to You
and sometimes it just feels good
to know You're there.

I know You're with me
when I'm feeling sad and lonely,
or when I'm scared.
And when I'm feeling happy
and having lots of fun,
I know You're smiling with me.

Thank You for sharing
my day with me.

You are like a best friend to me
because I know You're always listening.
I can tell You how I really feel,
even when I can't tell anyone else.
I can tell You when I'm mad or sad
and when I'm feeling lonely.

Sometimes grown-ups don't have time
to listen because they are busy.
That's why I'm so glad I have You.

Thank You for always listening
to what I have to say.

I like
baseball, bubble gum,
candy, race cars,
french fries,
nights without bedtimes,
days without rules,
dessert before dinner
and my very favorite pet.

I like lollipops
that are big and swirly,
sticky and sweet.
I like sharing them with someone,
or even a couple of someone's
because finding someone
who likes what You like
makes whatever You like
seem twice as good.

I like telling You
about the things I like.
It's my way of
saying thanks.

When I was little
there were a lot of things I couldn't do.

You helped me to grow
bigger and stronger.
I remember when I was too little
    to tie a bow.
Now, I can tie a bow
and do lots of other things by myself.

I hope it makes You happy
when I learn to do new things, God.
I hope it makes You proud of me.

I know how good
it makes me feel
when someone
shares with me.

Today I found out
how good it makes me feel
when I share
with someone else.

It was kind of funny
because I thought I would
feel like I had less
after I gave something away.
But do You know what, Father?
I felt like I had even more!

You give to us
in many ways, Dear Lord.
One way is through
other people.
Help me to be
one of Your
giving people.

I like to wonder
where the sun goes
when it gets dark...

I like to wonder
why I can see the moon
on some nights
and on some nights
I can't...

I like to wonder
what treasures lie hidden
deep on the ocean's floor...

There are a lot of things
I like to wonder about.
But I like *knowing*
that God is everywhere.

Thank You for today, God.
It was the perfect day
for playing with my friends.
We play lots of games together.
We play kickball,
and hide-n-seek,
and tag.

Sometimes when we play tag
I am "It."
Sometimes I laugh so hard
I can't run very fast.
I don't mind being "It" though,
because we always have
so much fun!

Thank You for my friends, God.
They help me in many ways.
Especially when we play tag,
because you can't play tag
alone.

I asked my Mom
how she knew
that love goes on forever.

She said that since
God is love
and God is forever
then love must be forever.

She said that my
great, great grandmother
knew Your love,
and that my
great, great grandchildren
will know Your love, too.

So, I guess that love
does go on forever
and that makes me
very happy!

One day I'll be grown up.
I'll get to dress up
whenever I want.
I'll get to do what I like
and go wherever
I choose to go.

Right now, it feels like it will be forever
before I grow up.

You have so much love
to give us, Father,
that You must have invented forever
so You would have enough time
to give it all
to us!

There are times when I think
I couldn't possibly
take another step.

Then my special friend
comes along and helps me.
He makes me laugh at
the funny things he shows me.
He makes me laugh at myself.
He doesn't get mad at me,
or call me names.
He likes me
because I'm me.

It makes me feel special.
It makes me feel like taking another step. . .
it even makes me feel like running!

And it makes me remember
the most special friend
I have is You, Father.

I'm thankful for all the things
I can do with my voice, dear God.

I can sing,
I can shout,
I can say the nicest things.

Sometimes I can whisper,
sometimes I can laugh,
and I love to whistle when I'm happy.

I love the voice You gave me.
Thank You, God.

Laughing
is a good feeling
that wells up
inside of us
like water in a fountain
until we feel so good
that it just overflows.

Thank You for laughter, God.
It's such a fun way
to share a good feeling.
It's such a fun way
to share Your love
for us.

Thank You for snow God,
my friends and I love
to play in it!
It makes everything
seem so fresh and clean!

Some of us
like catching the falling flakes
on the tip of our tongues!
And some of us
like making angels
in the snow!
But all of us like
making a snowman
together.

Thank You for the
cold outside
that brings the snow.
It always makes me feel so
warm inside.

When I am hurting
it feels like
the pain will
never go away.

But when my mom
gives me a band aid
and a hug
it makes me
feel better.

Thank You for
Your love Father.
It's kind of like
a big band aid
that makes everyone
feel better.

I like playing
hide-n-seek.
Because I hide
the best of all
my friends and
no one can
ever find me!

I like costume parties
because I get to
wear a costume
and a mask and
no one knows
it's me.

It would be hard to
play hide-n-seek
with You God
because You're everywhere!
And it would be even
harder to fool You
at a costume party
because You know everything!
Even behind my mask
You would know
it was me!

I wish I was alive
back in the time
when Jesus was first born.

I would have liked to
bring Him a present.
I would have brought Him
a warm furry bear
to cuddle with
in His cradle
in the stable.

Christmas is when
we celebrate Jesus' birthday.
It's a time when we give
to each other
so we can all remember
the special gift
Baby Jesus gave us all!

And it's a time when we can say,
"Happy Birthday Jesus!"

Sometimes when
my parents tell me
it's time to go to bed,
I get cranky
and start to whine.
Sometimes I even cry.
Then, I promise myself
I'm going to stay awake all night
just to show them
that I don't need
to sleep.

Then somehow
the next morning comes
without me remembering
how it got here.
I guess I do need
to sleep after all.

And it makes me feel
better to know that You know Lord,
that I don't mean to be mean
and cranky
at the end of the day. . .
it's just that I'm tired.

Sometimes I like
playing by myself.
That's the time
when I try to bring to life
the ideas I keep
tucked away in my imagination.

That's the time
I build castles from sand,
and airplanes from paper wrappers.

When I play alone
my castles stand tall,
my ships sail the seas,
my airplanes fly so high!

I think that's because
when I play alone
I feel very close to You, God...
and when I feel close to You
anything seems possible.

Sometimes I get very upset
when I make a mistake.

I think that I
have hurt Your feelings
by doing something
wrong.

Help me to understand
that Your forgiveness
gives me the chance
to try again.
Help me to know
with Your love
I can do better
next time.

If I look
very closely,
even the smallest things
in the world
show me
how great You are.

I think of You
when I see great big fluffy clouds,
I think of You
when I see mountains that seem
to touch the sky,
and I think of You
when I see one tiny flower
in the middle of a field.

Only You could make such
a perfectly beautiful flower
grow in a great big open field.

If I look
very closely,
everything in the world
shows me
how great You are.

Prayers and Devotions

THE SIGN OF THE CROSS

In the name of the Father,
and of the Son,
and of the Holy Spirit. Amen.

GLORY BE

Glory be to the Father
and to the Son
and to the Holy Spirit,
as it was in the beginning,
is now and ever shall be,
world without end. Amen.

GRACE BEFORE MEALS

Bless us, O Lord, and these Your gifts
which we are about to receive
from Your bounty
Through Christ our Lord. Amen.

GRACE AFTER MEALS

We give You thanks, O almighty God,
for all Your benefits;
You who live and reign,
world without end. Amen.

THE OUR FATHER

Our Father, who art in heaven,
hallowed be Thy name,
Thy kingdom come,
Thy will be done,
on earth as it is in heaven.
Give us this day our daily bread,
and forgive us our trespasses
as we forgive those
who trespass against us,
and lead us not into temptation,
but deliver us from evil. Amen.

THE HAIL MARY

Hail Mary, full of grace,
the Lord is with thee;
blessed art thou among women,
and blessed is the fruit
of thy womb, Jesus.
Holy Mary, Mother of God,
pray for us sinners now
and at the hour of our death. Amen.

GUARDIAN ANGEL PRAYER

Oh Angel of God
my Guardian dear
to whom God's love
commits me here.
Ever this day
be at my side
to light and guard
to rule and guide.
Amen.

The Sacraments

1. Baptism

2. Confirmation

3. Holy Eucharist

4. Reconciliation

5. Anointing of the Sick

6. Holy Orders

7. Matrimony

The Chief Spiritual Works of Mercy

To admonish the sinner.

To instruct the ignorant.

To counsel the doubtful.

To comfort the sorrowful.

To bear wrongs patiently.

To forgive all injuries.

To pray for the living
and the dead.

The Chief Corporal
Works of Mercy

To feed the hungry.

To give drink to the thirsty.

To clothe the naked.

To visit the imprisoned.

To shelter the homeless.

To visit the sick.

To bury the dead.

The Beatitudes

1. Blessed are the poor in spirit, for the kingdom of heaven is theirs.

2. Blessed are those who are sad, for they shall be comforted.

3. Blessed are the mild and gentle, for they shall inherit the land.

4. Blessed are those who hunger and thirst for justice, for they shall be filled.

5. Blessed are the merciful, for they shall receive mercy.

6. Blessed are the pure in heart, for they shall see God.

7. Blessed are those who make peace, for they shall be called the children of God.

8. Blessed are those who suffer for my sake, for heaven will be theirs.

The Ten Commandments

1. I, the Lord, am your God. You shall not have other gods besides me.

2. You shall not take the name of the Lord, your God, in vain.

3. Remember to keep holy the sabbath day.

4. Honor your father and your mother.

5. You shall not kill.

6. You shall not commit adultery.

7. You shall not steal.

8. You shall not bear false witness against your neighbor.

9. You shall not covet your neighbor's wife.

10. You shall not covet anything that belongs to your neighbor.

The Rosary

THE JOYFUL MYSTERIES

1. The Coming of Jesus is Announced
2. Mary Visits Elizabeth
3. Jesus is Born
4. Jesus is Presented to God
5. Jesus is Found in the Temple

THE SORROWFUL MYSTERIES

1. Jesus' Agony in the Garden
2. Jesus is Whipped
3. Jesus is Crowned with Thorns
4. Jesus Carries His Cross
5. Jesus Dies on the Cross

THE GLORIOUS MYSTERIES

1. Jesus Rises from His Tomb
2. Jesus Ascends to Heaven
3. The Holy Spirit Descends
4. Mary is Assumed into Heaven
5. Mary is Crowned in Heaven

Personal Record

Name_____

    born_____**in**_____

Baptism

    Date_____

    Priest_____

    Parish_____

    Godfather_____

    Godmother_____

First Communion

    Date_____

    Priest_____

    Parish_____

Confirmation

    Date_____

    Bishop_____

    Parish_____

    Sponsor_____

    Confirmation name_____

Family Record

Father_____

   born_____**in**_____

Mother_____

   born_____**in**_____

Brothers and Sisters_____

_____

_____

Father's family

  Grandfather_____

    born_____

  Grandmother_____

    born_____

Mother's family

  Grandfather_____

    born_____

  Grandmother_____

    born_____

This is my bed time prayer...

**This is my own prayer
thanking God for the day...**

This is my own prayer
thanking God for my friends...

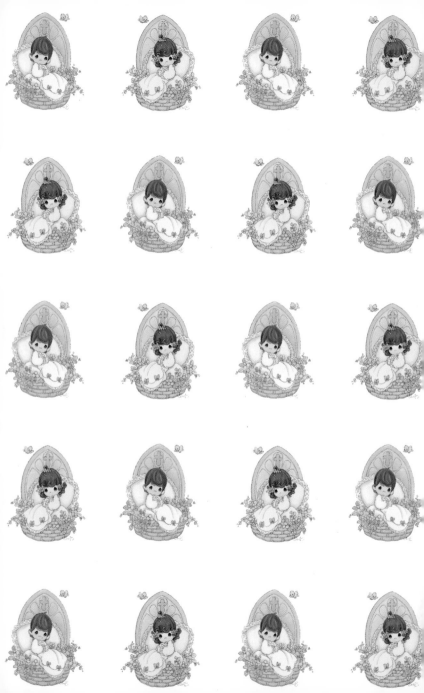